MW00582552

MUSCULAR SYSTEM

Natasha Vizcarra

Children's Press®
An imprint of Scholastic Inc.

Content Consultant
Greg Mack, ACE-CMES, ACE-CPT, CMSS
Educational Advisor, MedFit Education Foundation

Library of Congress Cataloging-in-Publication Data available
ISBN 978-1-339-02099-0 (library binding) | ISBN 978-1-339-02100-3 (paperback)

10 9 8 7 6 5 4 3 2 1   24 25 26 27 28

Printed in China 62
First edition, 2024

Design by Kathleen Petelinsek
Series produced by Spooky Cheetah Press

Find the Truth!

Everything you are about to read is true *except* for one of the sentences on this page.

Which one is **TRUE**?

T or F   *Charley horse* is another name for a muscle cramp.

T or F   All people can wiggle their ears.

Find the answers in this book.

What's in This Book?

Your face has 43 different muscles.

4

The **BIG** Truth

These tools can aid muscle recovery.

Teamwork!

Ouch! Muscle strain is a common injury.

INTRODUCTION

Plant one foot on the scooter. Push back with the other leg, and glide! In your body, a **team of muscles** in your kicking leg propels you forward. Hand **muscles help you grip** the handlebars. Other muscles shift your weight as you brace yourself to go downhill.

This is your **muscular system at work**—teams of muscles, **big and small**. You can feel them working. But did you know that there are other muscles in your body that you don't even notice you're using?

Your muscular system is made up of **three types of muscles**: **skeletal** muscle, smooth muscle, and **cardiac** muscle. They all work together to keep you moving and healthy. Read on to learn more about this amazing body system!

The word *muscle* comes from the Latin word *musculus*, which means "little mouse."

Lots of muscles work together when you ride a scooter!

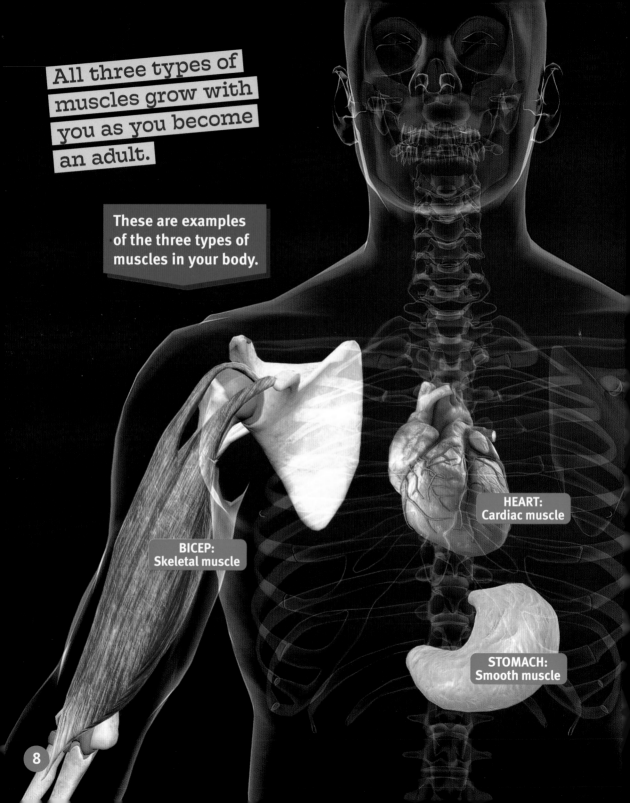

All three types of muscles grow with you as you become an adult.

These are examples of the three types of muscles in your body.

BICEP:
Skeletal muscle

HEART:
Cardiac muscle

STOMACH:
Smooth muscle

The Movement Makers

Your body contains a complex network of hundreds of muscles. These tough, elastic **tissues** perform different functions. Skeletal muscles hold your bones together and help you move around. Smooth muscles keep your internal **organs** and **blood vessels** working. Cardiac muscle in your heart pumps blood throughout your body. All your muscles have different functions, but they have one thing in common. They all work by **contracting**.

Contract, Relax, Repeat!

Muscles can only contract. And when the contraction is over, they naturally relax. For example, your hamstrings—the skeletal muscles at the back of your thigh—contract when you bend your knee. They relax when you straighten your leg. Smooth muscles in your intestines contract and relax to move food along. Your heart beats an average of 100,000 beats per day. Each beat is the result of your cardiac muscle contracting and relaxing.

You can feel your hamstrings at work when you do a squat.

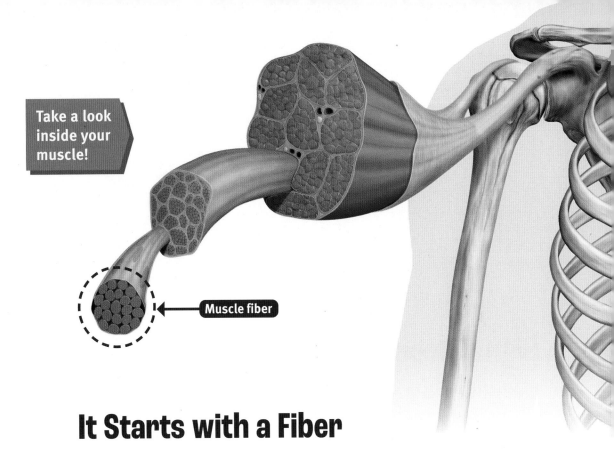

Take a look inside your muscle!

Muscle fiber

It Starts with a Fiber

A muscle may seem like a solid mass, but it's actually made up of many small **fibers** bundled together. Each fiber is a muscle cell that connects to a blood vessel and a neuron, or nerve cell. Blood vessels bring food and oxygen to nourish the fibers. They also carry away waste products like carbon dioxide and water. Neurons bring commands from your brain.

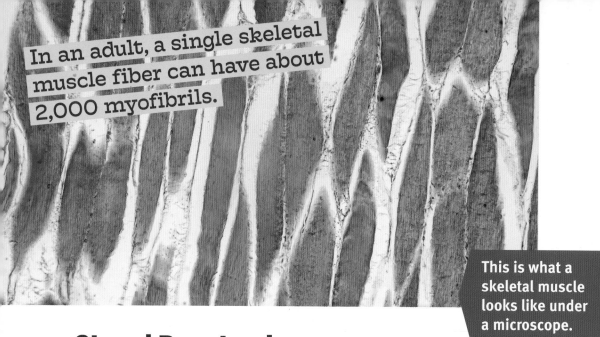

In an adult, a single skeletal muscle fiber can have about 2,000 myofibrils.

This is what a skeletal muscle looks like under a microscope.

Signal Received

Each fiber in a skeletal or cardiac muscle is formed by smaller units called myofibrils [mye-uh-FYE-bruhlz]. Each myofibril is divided into smaller sections called sarcomeres [SAHR-kuh-meerz]. When the brain sends a signal to a neuron connected to a muscle fiber, it causes segments in each sarcomere to slide toward one another. This shortens each sarcomere, contracting myofibrils and, ultimately, fibers, causing the muscle to contract.

Smooth muscle fibers don't have myofibrils or sarcomeres. They are much shorter than skeletal and cardiac muscle fibers. Long protein filaments called actin [AK-tin] span each smooth muscle fiber. Shorter filaments called myosin [MYE-uh-sin] connect to the actin on the ends of the cell. When the cells receive a signal to contract, myosin tug on the actin, causing the fibers to shorten and the muscle to contract.

This is what a smooth muscle looks like under a microscope.

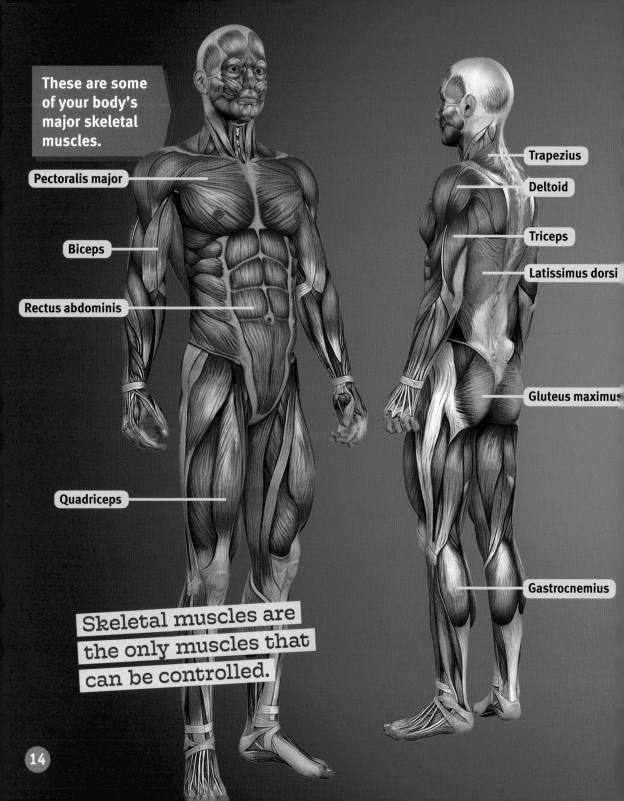

These are some of your body's major skeletal muscles.

Pectoralis major

Biceps

Rectus abdominis

Quadriceps

Trapezius

Deltoid

Triceps

Latissimus dorsi

Gluteus maximus

Gastrocnemius

Skeletal muscles are the only muscles that can be controlled.

CHAPTER

2

You're In Control

When you walk, run, or pick up your backpack, it's a voluntary action. That means you consciously choose to do it. Voluntary actions use our skeletal muscles. You have more than 600 skeletal muscles in your body. Examples include your chest muscles, calf muscles, and thigh muscles. Most skeletal muscles are connected to bones by tough cords of tissue called **tendons**. Others, like some muscles on your face, are connected to skin. Your skeletal muscles are hardworking. They need to rest after they've been in use for a long time.

Working Together

Many skeletal muscles that are connected to bones work in pairs. To lift your backpack, your arms use a pair of muscles called the biceps and triceps. Biceps are in the front of your upper arm. Triceps are in the back part. You grab the handle of your backpack. As your elbow bends to pull your lower arm upward, the contraction of your triceps lessens as your biceps contracts fully.

You also use your shoulder muscles every time you move your arm in an upward motion.

The tongue, a skeletal muscle, is actually made of eight separate muscles.

Super Support

Skeletal muscles aren't just for lifting things or moving around. Many of them are at work even when you are still. There are several groups of muscles in and around your **torso**, called your core muscles. They help you stand and sit up straight. More than 20 muscles in your neck support your head, which weighs about 12 pounds (5.4 kilograms). Muscles also protect your joints and hold them in place. For example, a triangular muscle called trapezius [truh-PEE-zee-uhs] anchors your shoulder blades to your spine.

Our longest skeletal muscles are the sartorius muscles. They run from the pelvis to the knees and let us sit cross-legged.

You use your butt muscles, among others, to walk.

From Biggest . . .

The biggest muscle in the human body is the gluteus [GLOO-tee-uhs] maximus. You have one in each butt cheek. When you are standing up, your glutes contract to keep your pelvis and upper legs stable. If you had weak butt muscles, other muscles would have to work extra hard to keep you upright.

... to Smallest

The smallest skeletal muscle is the stapedius [stah-PEE-dee-uhs]. When sound waves enter your ear, they vibrate your eardrum, then three small bones in your middle ear. The innermost bone, called the stapes [STAY-peez], generates a wave in the liquid of the inner ear. The stapedius muscle is connected to the stapes. If the sound is too loud, the stapedius pulls on the stapes to dampen the vibration before it reaches the inner ear.

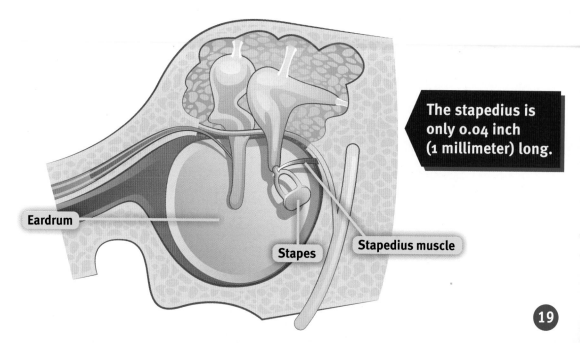

The stapedius is only 0.04 inch (1 millimeter) long.

Eardrum

Stapes

Stapedius muscle

Read My Face

We use our facial muscles to smile, frown, and express many other emotions. Some facial muscles connect to our skin. Others connect to our facial bones. Others are joined to one another. Because of these connections, even the slightest muscle contraction moves your facial skin. Combinations of these contractions result in different facial expressions.

The muscles in our face help us communicate with the world.

Wiggle Your Ears!

Give it a try! Don't feel bad if you can't do it. Ear wiggling is not a skill you can learn. The movement is controlled by auricular [oh-RI-kyuh-luhr] muscles, which are found just above the outer ear. Not all people have them. Millions of years ago, our ancestors had auricular muscles so they could move their ears toward a sound while staying absolutely still—like a cat does! Back then, people had to hunt for food—and hide from larger animals that could hurt them. Today we no longer need this ear-wiggling talent, so not everyone is born with these muscles.

Cats can rotate their ears 180 degrees. And they can move each one independently of the other.

Your pupils get larger in the dark and smaller when there's lots of light.

Your cardiac muscle gets a bit of rest when you're inactive, but it never stops working.

On Autopilot

When you walk into a dark room, what muscles are you using? If you said your leg muscles, you'd be right. But you might not have guessed that you're also using muscles in your eyes. Small muscles automatically **dilate** your pupils to let in more light. These muscles are involuntary muscles. They perform actions that you may not be aware of. Your body has two kinds of involuntary muscles—smooth muscles like your pupil dilator muscles, and cardiac muscle in your heart. Unlike skeletal muscles, smooth muscles and cardiac muscle can never fully rest.

Smooth Operators

Smooth muscles are found all over your body—mostly in your internal organs. For example, smooth muscles in your bladder make you go to the bathroom. Smooth muscles are also in your skin. When you're scared, surprised, or cold, smooth muscles called arrector pili [uh-REK-tuhr PYE-lye] in your hair **follicles** spring into action. They tug the fine hair on your skin upright. This causes tiny goose bumps to form on your skin.

Timeline: Muscular System Advances

1500s
Italian artist Leonardo da Vinci completes a sketchbook of human muscles.

1715
Dutch scientist Antonie van Leeuwenhoek observes tiny stripes in muscles.

1847
Swiss physiologist Rudolf Albert von Kölliker observes that some muscles are smooth.

1864
German physiologist Wilhelm Kühne extracts goo from ground-up muscle and names the protein myosin.

The Heart of the Matter

Cardiac muscle is found in the heart. This special kind of involuntary muscle is responsible for the heart's pumping action. When your heart contracts, it pushes blood out of its chambers and into your arteries. When your heart relaxes, blood returning from the body fills its chambers. That happens in a single beat, and your heart does it with enough force to move blood throughout your body.

Five to ten percent of an adult's weight is made up of smooth and cardiac muscles.

1954
Scientists discover how muscle fibers contract.

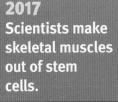

2017
Scientists make skeletal muscles out of stem cells.

2020
Scientists send mice to the International Space Station to study the effects of weightlessness on muscles.

TODAY
Researchers invent "wearable muscles" to help people with muscle **disorders**.

Picture This!

If you look at skeletal and cardiac muscles under a microscope, you would see that both are **striated**, which indicates the many individual muscle sarcomeres along a myofibril. These structures allow them to contract really fast and powerfully.

Smooth muscles don't have striations. Looking through a microscope, we can clearly see the cell nuclei, which appear as dark spots. We can barely see the fibers. Smooth muscles contract more slowly than skeletal and cardiac muscles. That makes smooth muscles ideal for slow, steady, and automatic processes like digestion.

With these you can compare how each type of muscle looks under a microscope.

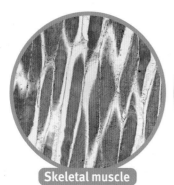

Skeletal muscle

Cardiac muscle

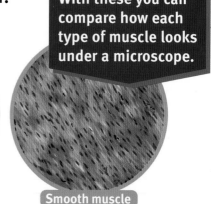

Smooth muscle

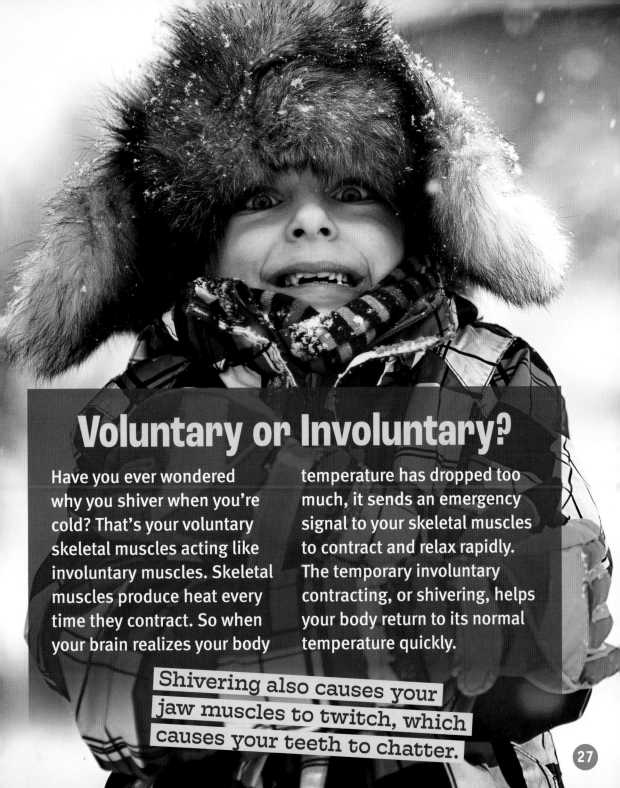

Voluntary or Involuntary?

Have you ever wondered why you shiver when you're cold? That's your voluntary skeletal muscles acting like involuntary muscles. Skeletal muscles produce heat every time they contract. So when your brain realizes your body temperature has dropped too much, it sends an emergency signal to your skeletal muscles to contract and relax rapidly. The temporary involuntary contracting, or shivering, helps your body return to its normal temperature quickly.

Shivering also causes your jaw muscles to twitch, which causes your teeth to chatter.

27

Teamwork!

The muscular system does not function on its own. Learn how it works together with many of the body's other systems to keep your body running.

Nervous System: →

Your muscles can't function without instructions from your nervous system. Your brain and spinal cord send commands—part electric, part chemical—to networks of nerves that connect to muscle fibers. Neurons in the fibers tell the muscle to contract. Or they stop sending a signal, which leads to the muscle relaxing.

Respiratory System:

Every time you breathe in, muscles in your rib cage and your diaphragm contract and your abdominal muscles relax. The opposite happens when you exhale. In turn, the oxygen provided by the respiratory system keeps your muscles working.

Nervous System

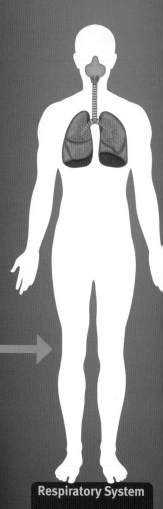

Respiratory System

Digestive System:

Your smooth muscles help your digestive system extract nutrients from food so your body can use them. In turn, your digestive system provides the nutrients your muscles—and the rest of your body—need to perform.

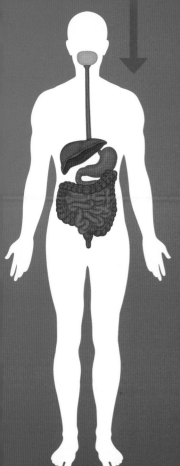

Digestive System

Circulatory System:

Muscles in your heart and blood vessels keep your circulatory system running around the clock. The circulatory system brings oxygen-rich blood to all your muscles and takes away waste.

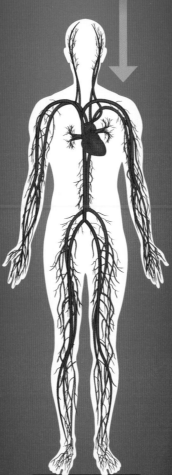

Circulatory System

Skeletal System:

The bones in your skeletal system work together with your muscles to keep you upright. They also work together to help you move.

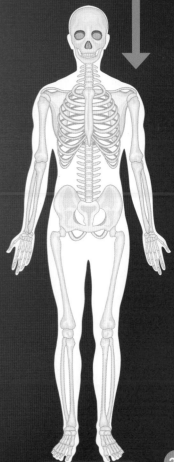

Skeletal System

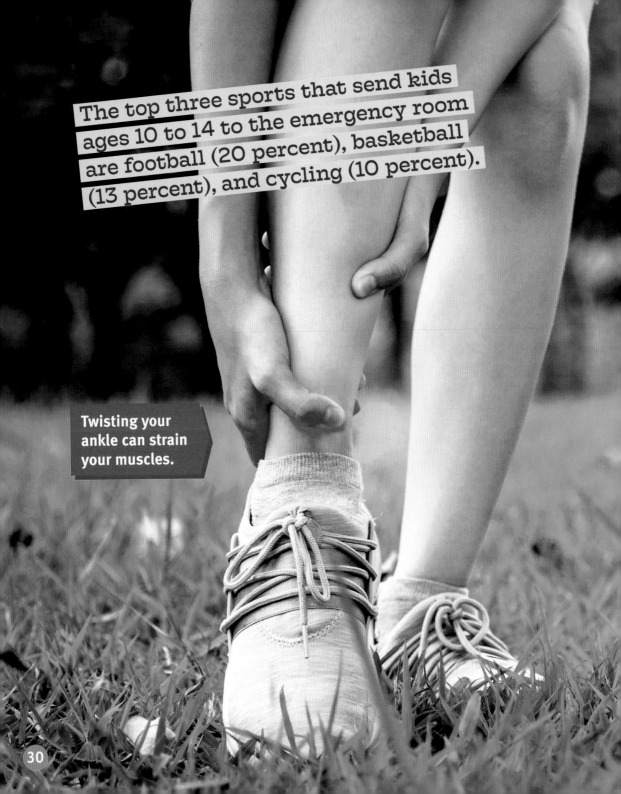

The top three sports that send kids ages 10 to 14 to the emergency room are football (20 percent), basketball (13 percent), and cycling (10 percent).

Twisting your ankle can strain your muscles.

When Muscles Hurt

When we think of getting hurt, we often imagine scraping our knee or fracturing an arm. But you can hurt your muscles too. Sometimes your muscles hurt because you overstretch them. For example, you may jump high to spike a volleyball, and when you come back down, your foot lands on a rock. You twist your ankle. Ouch! It's painful for days. Muscle injuries like a strained ankle are common. Let's look at other common injuries—and some more serious problems—and how they are treated.

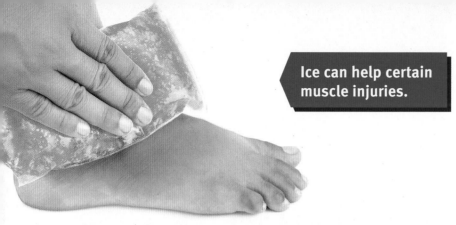

Muscle Strains and Muscle Fever

A strain happens when a person exercises beyond what their muscles can handle. It can be caused by sudden twisting or lengthening movements. A strain hurts immediately. There might be pain and swelling. It might be difficult to move the muscle for a few days. A muscle fever happens when someone attempts an exercise they aren't used to yet. That also causes aching, stiffness, and maybe swelling—but it happens 12 to 24 hours after the exercise. That's why it's also called Delayed-Onset Muscle Soreness, or DOMS. Strains and DOMS are treated at home with rest and ice.

Muscle Cramps

If you've ever been awakened by a cramp, you know it's painful! A muscle cramp is a sudden and involuntary contraction of one or more of your muscles. A cramp will usually go away on its own, especially if you relax and take deep breaths. To prevent cramps, drink plenty of water before and during exercise. You should also warm up before exercising vigorously.

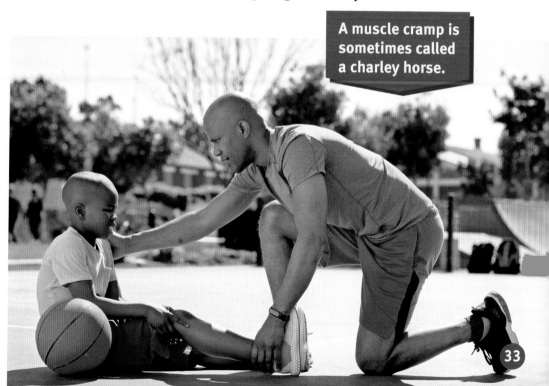

A muscle cramp is sometimes called a charley horse.

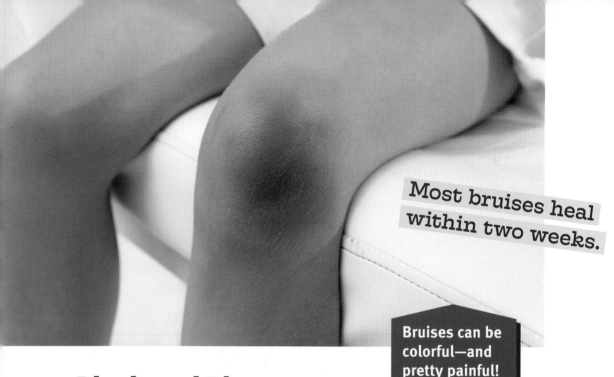

Most bruises heal within two weeks.

Bruises can be colorful—and pretty painful!

Black and Blue

A bruise happens when a blunt force, like a kick, blow, or fall, injures the muscles. There is immediate pain and swelling, and the injured part becomes black and blue over time. Bruises happen often in high-contact sports like football, ice hockey, and martial arts. Bruises may hurt, but they can usually be treated at home. Resting can help. If the pain doesn't go away after a few days, it's time to see the doctor.

Torn Muscles

Tears happen when a vigorous movement rips many muscle fibers or part of a tendon. They cause severe pain and swelling. Tears are serious injuries that should be immediately treated by a doctor. The doctor might prescribe a lot of rest, some anti-inflammatory medicine, and physical therapy. The tendon and muscle will heal and knit themselves back together over time. A physical therapist can recommend exercises that gradually strengthen the healing muscles or tendons.

Physical therapy can help recovery from a muscle tear.

ALS and Myopathy

Muscle disorders are less common than muscle injuries. They cause pain, weakness, and sometimes paralysis. Amyotrophic lateral sclerosis (ALS) and myopathy are two serious muscle disorders. As of today, there is no cure for either. ALS causes loss of muscular control. Myopathy can make a person so weak that daily activities like combing one's hair become difficult.

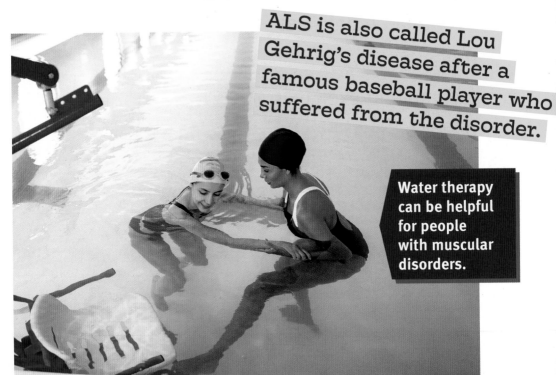

ALS is also called Lou Gehrig's disease after a famous baseball player who suffered from the disorder.

Water therapy can be helpful for people with muscular disorders.

Wearable Muscles

Scientists are always looking for ways to help people with muscle disorders. In 2022, researchers in Zurich, Switzerland, started testing wearable muscles—a kind of vest with cuffs for the arms. Sensors in the fabric detect the wearer's intended movements and relay data to a control box. The box then pulls or relaxes cables attached to the cuffs, causing the arm to move.

People with muscle disorders help test medical innovations.

Muscular Dystrophy

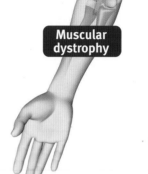

A comparison of muscles

Muscular dystrophy

Normal muscle

Muscular dystrophy is a genetic disorder, which means that it is inherited from a parent. Muscular dystrophy causes muscles to waste away. In 2021, researchers developed a promising new treatment that fixes the genetic mutation that slowly causes muscle cells to die. It can't help muscle cells already damaged by the disease, but it can prevent healthy cells from being affected. That's why researchers recommend the treatment for children immediately after diagnosis. The treatment is still being tested, but the hope is that it could someday change the lives of thousands of people.

A New Way of Moving

Petting a cat. Writing your name on a piece of paper. Taking a deep breath. Each of these seemingly simple actions is a fascinating team relay by hundreds of muscles in your body. All your muscles have different roles to play—and we're not even aware of much of the work they do! So give your muscular system a big thank-you. And make sure to take good care of it!

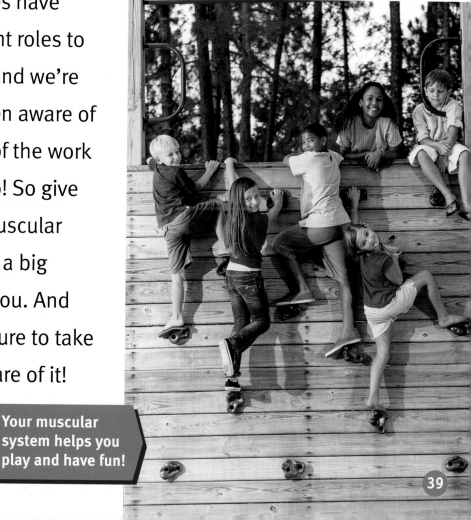

Your muscular system helps you play and have fun!

Muscular Care

Doctors, nurses, and physical therapists work with us to prevent and treat disease. Here are a few health care professionals who treat the muscular system, and some of the tests they may perform.

Checking posture

Stethoscope

Pediatrician: This doctor might give young patients a sports physical at their yearly checkup. In addition to listening to the heart with a stethoscope, the doctor will check a patient's posture, joints, muscular strength, and flexibility. This is also the first doctor to see for a muscle injury. If the injury is serious, this doctor will recommend that the patient see a specialist.

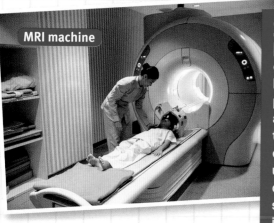
MRI machine

Physiatrist: A physiatrist [fi-zee-A-trist] is a doctor who diagnoses disorders of the muscles, nerves, bones, or brain. Among other things, a physiatrist examines the injured area and range of motion to understand how the injury affects the whole body. This doctor might test a patient's blood. To understand the extent of the injury, this doctor might also ask for imaging tests, such as X-rays, magnetic resonance imaging (MRI) scans, or computerized axial tomography (CAT) scans.

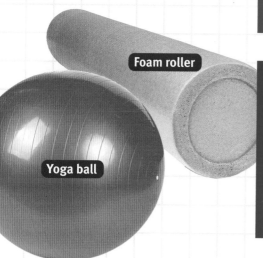
Foam roller

Yoga ball

Physical Therapist: A physical therapist takes a pediatrician's or physiatrist's diagnosis and chooses a set of exercises to treat the injury. Physical therapists, or PTs, help patients move and feel better. Patients see a PT frequently while in recovery—often weekly. A PT makes sure exercises are done properly and effectively.

Protect Your Muscular System

Keeping your muscular system healthy is important. And if you take care of it now, you will have a healthier future. Here are six things you can do to protect your muscles.

Exercise Regularly

When you are active, you move your muscles—and that makes them stronger. Weight-bearing exercises are great for building muscles. When you walk, run, or do push-ups and pull-ups, you carry your own weight. The same goes for planks and squats. No need for extra equipment!

Warm Up Before Exercising

Warming up gradually increases blood flow to your muscles. This prepares them for more vigorous exercise. Remember to cool down when you're done! To cool down, do 10 minutes of your activity slowly.

Drink Plenty of Water

When you exercise, your muscles heat up and they use up energy faster than usual. Water helps cool you down and delivers nutrients to your muscle fibers so you have the energy to keep going.

Eat a Balanced Diet

Carbohydrates fuel your muscles and are found in foods like rice and potatoes. Protein from sources like chicken, milk, lentils, and peanuts build and repair muscles. You don't need a lot of it, but fat helps your body absorb vitamins. Pick healthy sources of fat like avocados and nuts.

Wear Protective Gear in High-Contact Sports

Batting helmets and face guards protect your facial muscles. In sports like hockey or rugby, pads and guards protect your muscles from your neck down to your ankles. If you cycle long distances, padded shorts can protect your butt muscles.

Get Enough Rest

Exercising causes microscopic tears in your muscle fibers. When you rest, cells called fibroblasts [FYE-bruh-blasts] repair the tears. When your muscles heal, they become stronger.

True Statistics

Average number of times eye muscles move in one day: 100,000

Number of seconds it takes for eye muscles to shut your eyelids: 0.1

Average number of myofibrils in an adult's skeletal muscle fiber: 2,000

Number of seconds it takes for a muscle fiber to use up stored energy: 3

Percent of the body's blood flow that muscles receive during intense exercise: up to 80 percent

Percent of the body's blood flow that muscles receive when the body is resting: 20 percent

Did you find the truth?

T *Charley horse* is another name for a muscle cramp.

F All people can wiggle their ears.

Resources

Other books in this series:

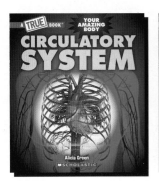 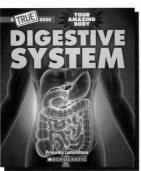  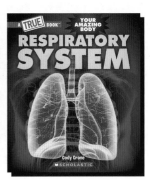

You can also look at:

Beevor, Lucy. *Understanding Our Muscles*. North Mankato, MN: Capstone Press, 2017.

Brett, Flora. *Your Muscular System Works!* North Mankato, MN: Capstone Press, 2015.

Farndon, John. *Stickmen's Guide to Your Mighty Muscles and Bones*. Illustrated by Venitia Dean. Minneapolis: Hungry Tomato, 2017.

Midthun, Joseph. *The Skeletal and Muscular Systems*. Chicago: World Book, 2014.

Simon, Seymour. *Muscles: Our Muscular System*. New York: Morrow Junior Books, 1998.

Glossary

blood vessels (BLUHD VES-uhlz) any of the tubes in your body through which blood flows

cardiac (KAHR-dee-ak) of or having to do with the heart

contracting (kuhn-TRAKT-ing) becoming smaller

dilate (DYE-late) to widen or become larger

disorders (dis-OR-durz) physical or mental illnesses

fibers (FYE-burz) strands of muscle tissue

follicles (FAH-li-kuhlz) small pouchlike cavities formed by a group of cells

organs (OR-guhnz) parts of the body, such as the heart or the kidneys, that have a certain purpose

skeletal (SKEL-uh-tuhl) of or having to do with the framework of bones that supports and protects the body of an animal with a backbone

striated (STRY-ay-tid) marked by alternating dark and light cross bands

tendons (TEN-duhnz) strong, thick cords or bands of tissue that join a muscle to a bone or other body part

tissues (TISH-ooz) masses of similar cells that form a particular part or organ of an animal or a plant

torso (TOR-soh) the part of your body between your neck and your waist, not including your arms; the trunk

Index

Page numbers in **bold** indicate illustrations.

About the Author

Natasha Vizcarra is a journalist and children's book author. She got to know her muscles well when she biked across the United States with other cyclists in 2002. Fifteen years later, her muscles amazed her again when she finished a marathon in Denver, Colorado. These days, she just likes to walk and hike. She lives near Boulder with her husband, Chris, and their cats, Rico, Pepe, and Krakee the Kraken. Read more about Natasha's writing at www.natashavizcarra.com.